Wiggle Room

Finding a Niche in Publishing Children's Books
Written by Rochelle O'Neal Thorpe

ISBN 978-1-935706-31-1
Library of Congress Control Number: 2010932826

Printed in the USA

Wiggle Room

Wiggle Room

TABLE OF CONTENTS

Introduction

This book is an introductory guide to help new writers and illustrators by answering frequently asked questions; it is not meant to be an authority on the publishing industry.
The chapters highlight a summation of experiences I have had since launching Wiggles Press in March 2009. Each chapter also includes contributions from authors, artists, and industry professionals who share their insights on topics related to publishing.

The amount of information related to publishing is vast and cannot be encompassed in one book.

There are several web sites and books to review for more comprehensive resources on writing children's books.

Here are a few:

20 Tips for Writing Children's Books (Pat Mora)
http://www.patmora.com/tips.htm

Aaron Shepard's Kidwriting Page
http://www.aaronshep.com/kidwriter

Society of Children Book Writers and Illustrators
http://www.scbwi.org

Independent Book Publishers Association
http://www.ibpa-online.org

Writing Children's Books for Dummies, by Lisa Rojany Buccieri and Peter Economy, Wiley Press

http://www.amazon.com/Writing-Childrens-Dummies-Rojany-Buccieri/dp/0764537288

WiggleRoom

Chapter 1. Where to Start

The most important things to keep in mind are your target audience and the underlying theme you wish to illustrate in the story.

Research
Take the time to review books at a library or bookstore for the age group you desire to address.

When reviewing these books, take note of the artwork, page count, and writing style; then decide whether you want to write rhymes or prose.

Word Count
Picture books range from one paragraph to 500 words.

Preschool story books range from 10 to 250 words. Picture books for kindergarten to first grade may range from 50 to 350 words.

Books for first to third grade readers can range from 100 to 500 words.

Books for 9 to 14 year olds can range up to 1,000 to 2,000 words. Consider a chapter book or short story novel for young readers for any count higher than 2,000 words.

Character Building
When writing a book for children it is important to consider the main characters, themes, timeline,

scenes and book size. Writing a draft and creating a description for each character will help the author, as well as communicate expectations to the artist developing illustrations later on.

Drafting a story board that includes the characters and scenes of the book will help the author to follow a consistent theme and to visualize the development of the story as well.

Character Descriptions
Determining how each character will be presented helps the author determine the age, height, weight, sex, and personality of the main characters.

Scene or Setting
Deciding on a contemporary, futuristic or historic setting will also develop the scene for the artist to follow when drafting the sketches for the book.

Writing Style
The first drafts of most novice writers will need editing. It is important to join writing groups and to hire an experienced editor to review your drafts to help refine your work. If the story is well written, the publisher will often help with story development; however, most publishers prefer submittals of clean (edited) copy.

Poetry or Prose
Poetry is fun and children love rhyme. Books by Dr. Seuss, for example, are really popular for early childhood readers.

However, writing rhymes and poetry that communicate a full thought and story doesn't come easily for most people.

Readers enjoy stories with well-developed characters and these stories need little narration to guide the reader. A theme that is evident through the actions of the main characters and inspires the imagination is a story that can come alive with illustration and color.

If you have to narrate every line or preach to teach, the copy or story is missing key elements that engage the reader's imagination.

For example:

A: The rabbit tasted the soup and decided he would rather go hungry ...

B: The rabbit took one sip from the bowl. *Yuk, this soup is horrible.*

Although these sentences are similar, the approach is very different: example A narrates, while example B communicates the character's thoughts and actions.

Short Story or Novel

Stories that exceed 1,000 words may be developed further to create a chapter book or children's novel, especially if there are a number of characters engaged in dialogue and several scenes of action.

Often, an inspired author knows that a story they are writing could be developed into a series. Instead of an individual story, the author can combine several stories into a chapter book for preteens or teen readers.

Juvenile chapter books can be as little as 60 pages, which is like combining two 32 page books. A chapter

---

book may be a better option than publishing several small picture books which are heavy in text.

Artwork

Children's books require illustrations, which impact both page length and publication costs. The cost of illustrations can range from $25 to $100 per page depending on the artist's experience and/or desire to work on your project.

Some experienced artists will negotiate the price for a project ranging from $10 to $30 per page, and some will not negotiate at all. Very popular illustrators can charge as much as $3,000 to $5,000 for a picture book.

Some artists will want the option to make royalties from the published work, and others prefer to be paid a higher flat flee and not depend on royalties to earn their revenue. On average, artists want a reasonable fee plus royalty income.

Artists will prefer a flat fee for books by new authors just entering the industry whose work might be harder to sell.

Many traditional or commercial publishing houses have their own lists of illustrators and artists and may assign an artist to the project without offering the author the option of choosing or selecting an artist. Therefore, the author may have very little control over the selection of an artist or book design.

Publishers own the rights to artwork they commission or pay for on behalf of an author. The author only owns the text or copy of a book.

Wiggle Room

Authors who self-publish or want to control the visuals of the artwork should communicate this to their publisher.

When subsidizing the cost of artwork, it is important for the author to contract with the publisher for the rights to the artwork and to determine prior to publishing a book who has ownership of the images.

Original artwork is often the property of the artist and ownership of the art remains with the artist who then grants the author or publisher the right to use the artwork for the publication of the book.

If you want to own the artwork, you must pay for the completed artwork and contract with the artist for ownership rights.

Should the author commission artwork directly, the artwork and images should be copyrighted by the author to secure ownership and the right to use the artwork in the book and related marketing.

The author should make it clear in the contract that the illustrations cannot be sold or utilized in other publications.

The key to success is drafting an agreement that clearly defines the rights and obligations of the publisher, author and artist.

Editing
The most important thing is to find a good editor that you can work with and enjoy.

Submit the copy to the editor for corrections without illustrations and later include the illustrations for his or

WiiggleRoom

her review to make sure the copy is consistent and that the images or sketches bring the story alive. An editor can help ensure that key elements to the story are not missed in print or visually in the artwork.

Allow time for review and communicate even the smallest change to the production team.

It takes time to incorporate changes and any change will affect your timeline or deadlines for publishing the book.

Frequently Asked Questions

How do I submit a book?
Review the website of your desired publisher for their specific directions.

Books are commonly submitted in the following ways:

- Direct Submissions: this means sending a manuscript by mail with a copy of the manuscript and a self-addressed stamped envelope so the publishers can send it back with a reply.
- Literary Agents: this means that the author hires an agent who has built relationships with that publisher.

Who should illustrate the book?
Most publishers do not accept manuscripts with illustrations. They usually assign projects to in-house artists or freelancers.

Small publishing houses will accept books submitted with illustrations because it reduces their costs. However, if the work isn't already finished, a small publisher will still want the ability to authorize, approve and revise the art produced for a production they will publish.

Completed Artwork:

When submitting a book with the artwork completed, the author and illustrator have already worked out the costs (author has paid the artist).

Even when the author has paid or will pay the artist, the publisher is not obligated to accept the work and retains the right to approve what will be published.

The publisher should be sent sketches as well as artwork for approval.

Text Only Submissions:

Prior to submitting your text to a contracted artist, the author should provide the publisher with the following:

1) Character Descriptions: include a page detailing hair and skin color, age, height, weight and other characteristics of the main character, even if it's a tree, animal, or robot.

2) Timeline: indicate whether it's winter, spring, summer, fall, day and/or night or other time periods.

3) Scene Descriptions: indicate village, town, bedroom, curtains, chairs, dress color, etc. This helps the artist to interpret the storyline.

Sketches are sent to the author for approval. Once sketches are approved – no edits can be made without incurring additional cost for producing new images.

Finding A Niche in Publishing Children's Books

What does a contract include?

If your work is accepted by a publisher, you will receive a contract. Authors should look over contracts with their attorney, especially if movie rights, electronic rights and foreign rights are involved.

The basic things included in contracts are:

1. Royalties
2. Rights: artwork, copy, and foreign
3. Publishing Date

Will I be in paperback or hardcover?

1) Hardcover: in the past most books were printed in hardcover and then released in paperback. This was because libraries and bookstores prefer hardcover for its longevity and shelf-life. Because library books pass through many hands, it was important to libraries to have durable books.

   However, today, with e-books and several electronic formats for books and the shrinking budgets of libraries and independent book dealers, paperback is becoming the norm. They are less expensive and paperback is a great way to test the market or popularity of an author without incurring huge costs.

2) Paperback: A book with great sales in paperback may be offered a limited edition in hardcover to test sales, or during the holiday season because it is popular.

Wiggle Room

Emerging Trends

It is important to research and become familiar with emerging trends in publishing.

Today, the big debate is over Internet Applications (Apps), and the use of electronic Apps for publishing books to be read on iPhones, iPad, Kindle, PDF Readers and through animation.

New software for converting stories to presentations for animation is being developed by such companies as Fablevision and Apple, as well.

Many writers are posting animated books and videos to YouTube to attract audiences.

Large publishing houses jumped on the bandwagon by partnering with Apple and HP to create bookstores like the Apple bookstore with Barnes & Noble, or Kindle bookstores with Microsoft and HP.

Animation software developers like FabelVision sold millions of books using an animated application for a children's story.

A book deal for the story was offered to FabelVision after it made the story available for free in order to publicize its App. With this success, it now charges up to $14,000 for use of the application, making it virtually impossible for independent or small companies to have access to such technology.

Once it hits mainstream or a volume of usage, consumer demand and competition should drive the cost down.

Wiggle Room

In fact, several small firms have already begun soliciting authors for manuscripts on Craigslist for testing their Apps and developing their users.

Sites like Engadet.com are a great source for learning about technology, and joining LinkedIn's Publishing Group will keep you in tune with the debates happening within the children's publishing industry.

Recent discussions have been about whether or not electronic books will drive down the demand for print and whether to self-publish or not.

You can be sure that writers still want the prestige of being offered a deal from a traditional publisher (TP). This has traditionally been the prestigious right of passage that validates and distinguishes the worthiness of an author.

However, everybody loves a winner so if you self-publish something and it sells, a traditional publisher will be in pursuit. Likewise, if software and electronic presentations drive sales, traditional and commercial publishers will find a way to corner that market too.

It is only to your benefit to be part of that conversation, so join a writers association or online group to stay abreast of emerging trends.

Chapter 2. Have a Passion for Writing

Inspiration

Writers are gifted people whose ability appears to come naturally, as if inspired by muses.

However, being creative requires a passion that needs to be nurtured as well.

It is important to set aside time to write down ideas that stir your imagination and to listen to your heart when developing characters and scenes that tell your story. It requires spending time alone writing and writing.

Joining writing groups and swapping copy with fellow writers is also a good way to test a story before it is presented to a publisher. You can test the market for your story by submitting a proposal versus the entire manuscript.

In fact, one story I received in a proposal format this year ended up being something the author and I collaborated on to make contemporary for this era and recent events.

It was a joy to work with the writer to inspire a new perspective for his story.

Another way to stay motivated is to read recently published children's books and reviews on new writers.

Several websites have reviews of new books, and bookstores today often have cafes where you can flip through a book off the shelf while drinking a cup of coffee.

By attending a book signing for a new author you can get a pulse of the market. Reviewing new books helps to get a view of the trends in the market regarding what is being published as well as current art design.

The most important thing is to be in touch with your target audience. Having young children at home makes this easy because children, grandchildren, nieces, nephews and neighborhood kids can tell you what they read, who they like and what shows they must see or have on DVD.

When I get several submissions I will read them to my five year old and let him tell me which story he likes. A story that captures his interest and has no pretty pictures is a good story.

Think of new ways to teach timeless lessons. When writing, think of what a child will learn from your story or take away as a life lesson.

If your goal is humor, think of what it is you want to help a child release through laughter.

For example, my eldest child was a perfectionist, so much so that if he made a single mistake, he would destroy the art or paper he was working on.

When I found the story **Regina's Big Mistake**, written by Marrisa Moss, I was so relieved to have an impersonal way to approach his frustration. Through this gentle, loving story about a little girl just like him, I

---

could hold up a mirror for my son and have a tool for resolving a problem by discussing this story together.

Recently, I discovered a book called **Kenya's Word**, by Linda Trice while sitting in the lobby of my pediatrician's office.

After reading the book, I just had to buy a copy for my son and my neighbor's child who were at the tender age when children become aware of race. **Kenya's Word** was a beautiful way to approach racial identity for children without judgment or focusing on differences. It was a wonderful find.

It was the following words from the Bible that inspired me to start Wiggles Press:

Ps 107:19,20
19 Then they cry unto the Lord in their trouble, and he saveth them out of their distresses.

20 He sent his word, and healed them, and delivered them from their destructions.

These words written by David the Master Poet inspired me to see that God can inspire writers. That through His spirit an author is able to write words that can heal a broken heart or place aspirations in the heart of a young one.

Words are powerful.
Although children's stories are not often religious or spiritual in nature, they influence a child's soul with the same depth.

My goal is to help writers produce stories that inspire, heal, and bring laughter to children and their parents or caregivers who read to them.

Editing

Once you have created the draft of your story, it is important to have someone else edit and critique it for consistency. If your writing is like mine, spelling and grammar will need careful attention and several revisions.

Yes, even the most inspired writer may not be a wordsmith – while writing, creative people are often more focused on ideas and imagination than on the details of grammar and punctuation. Editors can make sure your creative ideas make sense to the world and that your prose is readable.

The editor that is right for you will correct your grammar and edit content with an attempt to keep your unique voice and writing style.

An editor that squeezes the life out of your text and turns it into a news report or article is not right for creative writers.

The editor you choose to work with should have experience with children's publishing because their knowledgeable support of your career will help you stay motivated and well informed.

WiggleRoom

INSIGHTS FROM AN EDITOR
Ten Key Things to Consider
by Editor Eugenie Nakell

1. Use spell check (such a simple thing, but authors don't seem to do this);
2. Look at published adult and children's books to see how quotations are correctly formatted;
3. "That" refers to animals and objects; "who" refers to people (e.g., "I love the dog that lives next door" vs. "My friend Pete, who lives next door, is very tall");
4. If you are using a poetry format, each word at the beginning of a line is capitalized; if that doesn't work because of the placement of illustrations, the continuing line should be indented;
5. Capitalizing daddy and mommy (or grandparent, etc.) rule is: If addressing daddy or mommy, capitalize (e.g., "Hey, Mommy, you look nice"). If referring to daddy or mommy, do not capitalize (e.g., "His daddy was the best cook");
6. Minimize the use of semi-colons in children's books;
7. Phrases should be followed by a comma (e.g., "On the first day of the week, Sarah wore pink socks");
8. Names should be separated by commas (e.g., "Hi there, Pete, how is your day going?");
9. Be consistent in your punctuation and grammar;

10. Google words and phrases to see what is correct (e.g., when to use "in to" and when to use "into"). Just type the two choices in the search box, click, and the answers will come up.

INSIGHTS FROM AN AUTHOR
Paula M. Ezop Discusses Writing

I've always enjoyed doing the creative things in life: gardening, watercolors, writing, and any form of creative expression that allows me to express myself. I love colors, a fresh tube of paint, and the palette of colorful flowers that can fill a garden. I enjoy writing from my heart and soul, sharing the imaginative as well as the realities of life.

My writing is not limited to children's stories. I also write a spiritual column, "Following the Spiritual Soul," and my first published book, which was co-authored, was **Spirituality for Mommies**. And, through each of those writing experiences, I've learned something...I've grown not only as a writer but as a person.

My writing has put me in touch with some wonderful people. We enter each other's world through the written word, we learn from each other, and we grow professionally and in unseen, heartfelt ways.

As writers, we learn many things. We learn the joy of success and the sadness of disappointment and rejection.

But is success all that matters? Or is it the fact that you can touch another person's heart with your words? Is it the fact that you can make a small child smile or giggle, the way that only a child can? Or is it something as simple as creating something for others to enjoy, something that comes deep from within?

Following are some thoughts on what I've learned as a writer...

1. I remember something that I read years ago, and I've seen the same thought expressed by several authors since then. When asked about how they became a successful writer, a well-known author basically said, "I never quit, even though I received rejection after rejection – I never gave up. Don't give up on your dream. Keep writing and eventually you will find success." I've remembered that always and I've never given up on my dream...

2. Don't take rejection notices personally. Although I can write those words, rejection still doesn't come easy for me.

3. Finding an agent or a publisher isn't always the right answer. The agent or publisher who accepts your work needs to be just as passionate as you are about your writing and the work that you have created. Without their enthusiasm and belief in you, success will elude you.

4. Sometimes timing is everything – something you wrote several years ago may suddenly become sought after.

5. A contract doesn't always mean success. I have had two online companies accept my work. One company never fulfilled their contractual agreement. In fact, they are no longer online and never communicated to me

that they were going out of business. My manuscript was never published.

The second company published my children's book online but never marketed it in any way – for three years the story was online and not one sale.

Publishers may accept your work but it doesn't always mean success. I had no way of knowing this when I accepted these offers – I was just thrilled that my work was going to be published. But, I did learn from this experience.

6. Distribution and marketing are the keys to success. Without distribution, your book will never be a success. Make sure that the publisher has distribution plans in place and is extremely knowledgeable about marketing.

As I reflect upon what I have learned as a writer these words come to mind. "Writing for me is a journey of the heart and soul. I've written of the joys and the extreme sadness in my life. I've written to make children smile, wonder, and question. I've gone to that magical place where all things are possible, and I've loved every minute of it."

So, write just for the joy of writing, write to make a difference, write to share your wisdom, and write to entertain. Your writing is part of your personal journey…

WiggleRoom

Chapter 3. Artwork: Illustrating Picture Books & Novels

The average picture book is anywhere from ten lines of text to 500 words, ranging from 24 to 32 pages in length.

What brings a story to life and determines its size or length is, of course, the artwork.

Most children's books are brightly illustrated and include imaginative images that reflect the story without overshadowing the text. It is a marriage of words and images.

There are classics like **The Giving Tree**, by Shel Silverstein that have no color and utilize simple black and white drawings to tell his ever-poignant lesson of a selfless apple tree and a boy as he grows into manhood. Shel Silverstein's success with **The Giving Tree** has made black and white illustrations part of his brand and shows that a well-written story may not need color.

When creating page layouts, here are a few examples of what I have experienced with illustrations and artists. I hope they will help artists keep in mind the steps needed to produce something that will be enjoyed by all.

1. Read The Story
It is important for the artist to read the story over and over until they become as familiar with it as possible.

More often than not, I have gotten illustrations that leave out precious details that are written in the story;

after artwork has been completed, it is very hard to happily revise images. Egos get bruised easily. A simple read prevents these mistakes.

For example, if the writer states, "The book she brought home from school was titled **The Mystery of the Haunted House**, and then the artist draws an illustration of the child holding a book that says, **The Haunted House Mystery**, it means either changing the art or editing the book to reflect the artist's mistake. It is unfair to the author to have to re-write or edit a book because the artist wants to do their own thing.

The artist's job is to read and interpret the story to give it life and when this is done both authors and publishers are excited and readers will be too.

2. Decide Upon the Orientation of the Book
The next most important thing to consider is the orientation of the book. For example, 8 x 10 books are 8 inches in width and 10 inches in height. Illustrations should be 8.5 x 10.5 in size for printing to allow for bleeds and trim size.

Binding a book will take up .25 inch of a page. If a book is square, and therefore equal on all four sides, the artwork should be square as well (single pages), or the size of a two-page spread should be double the cover size, reflecting two open pages side by side.

A two-page spread for a 10 x 10 cover would be 20 x 10, or 20 inches in width 10 inches in height. For an 8 x 10 cover, the spread would be 16 x 10. Most spreads are centered on 17 x 11 tabloid pages.

Here is an example of a two-page spread on a 17 x 11 spread:

The artist left space for text to be inserted on the left page and the spread can be equally divided into two pages of equal size.

This same spread can also be converted into two 8 x 10 pages.

This artwork was designed by Michelle Podgorski, illustrator for ***Animal of the Year***, by Donald Cantor and Michael Cantor.

Here is a second example of a full page spread with room for text:

However, in the next image below the artwork dominates the page and leaves little room for the text of a story that is heavy in content. The image could have been reduced to leave more space for blending the art with the story.

Sketches by Allison M. Healy for **The Tales of Teacups**, written by Rochelle O'Neal Thorpe.

In the end, the book was designed with pages that alternated art on a page with text on the other to give the artwork full visibility without crowded text.

3. Characterizations & Guidelines

Most authors are requested to draft *character descriptions* of the personalities that will appear in the artwork.

Character descriptions should list identifiers like age, height, weight, hair color, complexion and any scene settings related to the location or timeline. This will give the artist a guideline for developing character sketches and the scenes in the background of their work.

This is a time for the artist and author to collaborate on their expectations for the imagery and style of the illustrations.

WiggleRoom

Artwork by Rosemarie Gillen

When developing a character for a story, the publisher needs to know what the author expects. The more details you can provide the better; for example, whether the characters should have certain racial features or clothing styles.

Sometimes a publisher will make changes to a character in a story that has been submitted. A publisher may desire to reach a target audience and opt to change the racial features of a character to expand the appeal of the book to multicultural audiences.

Here are examples of character changes:

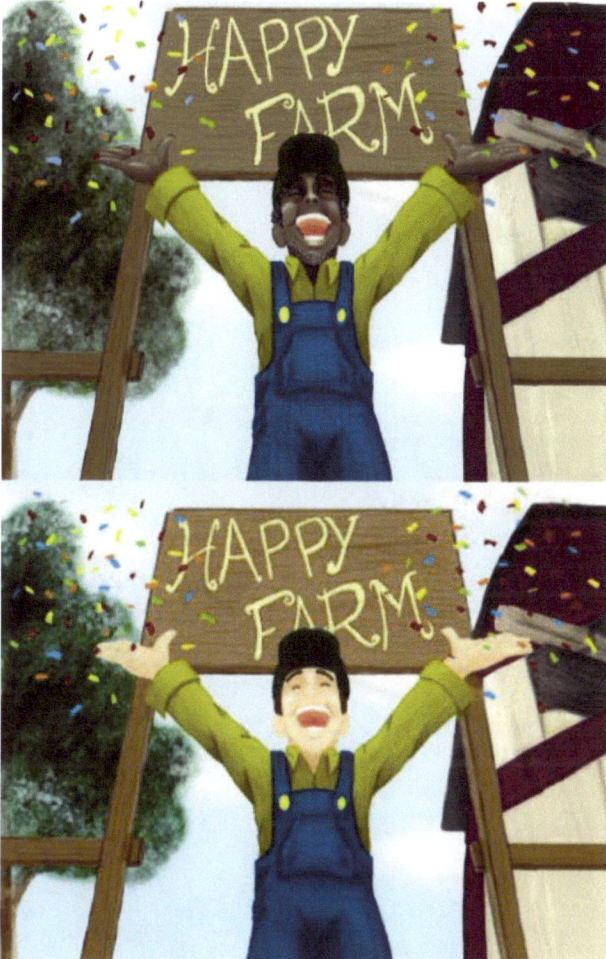

***The Perfect Pet, by Donald Cantor and Michael
Cantor and illustrated by Martin McDonald***

The farmer in the story was to be African-American
while the artist assumed he would be European.

It was very valuable that the artist could make the change and also deliver an African-American farmer with realistic features who was attractive and satisfied the goals of the author and publisher.

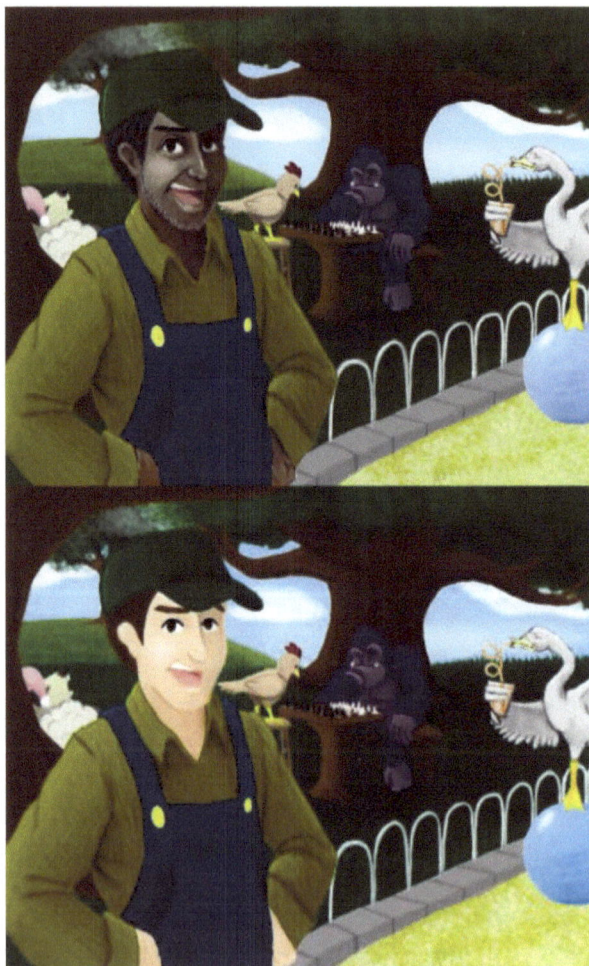

The Perfect Pet, by Donald Cantor and Michael Cantor and illustrated by Martin McDonald

WiggleRoom

4. Style
It is also important to know the different styles of artwork you can choose for your book:

Animation – a creative interpretation of a book that is comical and creative.

Realistic – a creative interpretation that mirrors real life, or portrait-style art – for serious, non-fictional stories.

Interpretive or Abstract – the artist can create imaginative and modern art forms to tell a story.

3 D – more dimensional and fantasy-style art seen in 3D movies or animation.

Animae – a style associated with Japanese Animation popularized by Dragon Ball Z and other famous Japanese animators.

Comic Strip – a style utilizing dream or idea boxes usually used with comic strips in comic books and newspapers.

Authors should research books and provide samples when possible of the style of artwork they want to produce.

5. Alternating Text
Some authors want fully illustrated stories but can't afford to pay for 32 pages of artwork. As a result, one option is to cut the number of pages of illustrations to half the page count of the book.

For example, if the story is a 32 page book, only 16 pages will have artwork. Some stories are better

Finding A Niche in Publishing Children's Books

Page **31** of 104

served by alternating text with illustrations because the story is a poem with few lines and needs images to increase the length of the book.

Here is an example of a story that has an illustration following the text page.

Why…there's Wally our whale!
Come and watch him spout!
When he's up a creek, he plays tag with the trout.

He's friendly and fun, and just as big as a house.
But he'll swim out to sea at first sight of a mouse.

The Perfect Pet, by Donald Cantor and Michael Cantor and illustrated by Martin McDonald.

6. Text Overlay

Below is an example of art designed for a children's book that leaves room for text and is created with an illustration that is animated and colorful. Spot colors allow the scene to come alive and leave ample room for text.

This also was a two-page spread converted to a single page for the printer's format.

They told her that Daffodil Day
was an annual affair,
where locals decorate everything
with the flower, even girls hair.

When we arrived on Nantucket
the street was full of people,
from the dock, to the town library,
and a white church with a steeple.

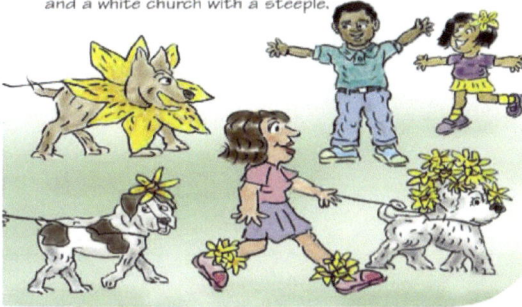

Gabe's Nantucket Adventure, by Rochelle O'Neal Thorpe and illustrated by Al Margolis

7. Text Wrap Around

The artist below created a page that was full-bleed; however, it had no space left for imported text. Therefore, the illustration was then reduced in size to fit within the page to make room for text above the image. If the full bleed had been used for each illustration, the page count would have increased and the book would have many text pages. Text wrap around is ideal for a content-heavy book.

I Guess My Mom Is Pretty Special, by Ann M. Logan and illustrated by Bill Young

8. Text with Frames

Sometimes authors want the text of a book framed on the page. This works nicely when the page of the book has a consistent or equal word count on each page of text in a book.

Often the artwork is also framed to make the book consistent in style.

When framing text, it is important to consider the word count from page to page. When text is heavy on one page and light on another, the variation in text can make a book look unbalanced.

When writing a book, authors seldom consider the book layout until after the book is in production.

Making page breaks in your document where scene changes occur will enable the author to review word count page by page. This will ensure a consistent flow prior to submitting a book for production. Dividing the total word count by page length is a useful way to determine an average word count per page.

For example: 1,000 words for a 32 page book will have an average word count of 32 words per page.

If the book is a poem or prose and you want to have alternating pictures, then 32 to 50 words per page will make the book look balanced.

If you are writing a book with alternating pages and the text is heavy, then cut the pages in half and recalculate the word count.

For example: 1,000 words for a 32 page book with heavy text would mean 1,000 divided by 16 pages instead, resulting in 62 to 100 words per page on average.

For chapter books and novels, this isn't the case because few, if any, images will be inserted.

9. Background Setting

Wiggle Room

When text is imported into an image or will be overlaid, it is important to consider if the text will be clearly visible.

Consider whether the background will require a change in font style, font color, point size or orientation of the text layout to be clearly visible for readers.

The white background in the first picture (Picture 1) below allows the text to stretch across the page in a simple color. This background also allows the designer to choose any font color.

Next was an owl from an island named Long.
He played himself in a game of ping pong.

Picture 1

The second image (Picture 2) limits the orientation of the text because of the building in the background. Also, the text colors must be visible on green grass.

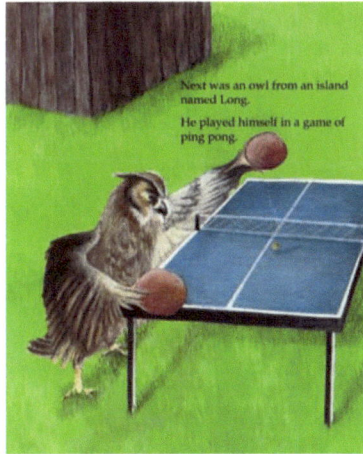

Picture 2

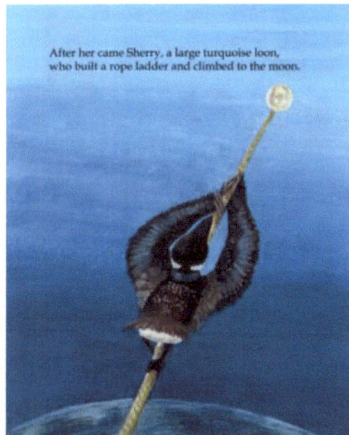

Picture 3

The third picture (Picture 3) allows for the text to span the page; however, the color of the font is limited by what will be visible against a blue background.

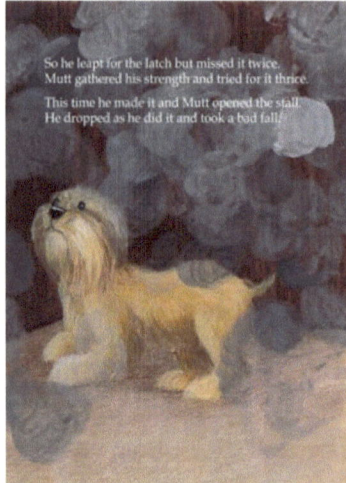

So he leapt for the latch but missed it twice.
Mutt gathered his strength and tried for it thrice.

This time he made it and Mutt opened the stall.
He dropped as he did it and took a bad fall.

Picture 4

Animal of the Year, by Donald Cantor and Michael Cantor and illustrated by Michelle Podgorski (images 1 to 4).

In the fourth image (Picture 4) a light font was needed in order to see the text on the background.

10. The Cover Art

What Should the Cover Include?

The cover art should include an image of the main character and a key or pivotal scene that relates to the book's title. Book covers are often designed after all the sketches are done and then selected from the artwork prepared for the book's interior.

However, on occasion, a cover will be designed separately and will not be derived from interior art.

The publisher may want to illustrate something unique about the main character or dramatize the theme of the story in the cover art.

Wiggle Room

The cover art design must consider space necessary for the title of the book as well as the author and illustrator names.

Most covers are a full-spread to include the back cover.

The publisher will want to include a brief book description and, on occasion, a paragraph about the author and the author's photo on the back cover.

Back covers must also incorporate the publisher's logo or imprint and the ISBN barcode assigned to the book.

WiggleRoom

INSIGHTS FROM AUTHOR GEORGE SOMMERS:
Turning a Nonfiction Story into a Creative Educational Experience

George Sommers' manuscript for *I SAW WILD PARROTS IN NEW YORK CITY!* included actual photography of wild (technically feral) parrots in Brooklyn, NY! This fact-based story explores the mystery of how parrots from a South American tropical rainforest arrived, adapted and thrived in the "wilds" of the Big Apple.

Illustrator Bill Young morphed those photos into colorful and wildly imaginative characters and scenes sure to appeal to the younger set. The synergy between author and artist results in a fun book with some interesting lessons about nature and the environment seamlessly woven in.

Older readers are sure to appreciate the "Parrot Paparazzi" section featuring the author's original photography - and the Question and Answer section on parrots both pets and wild.

- George P. Sommers

Here are examples:

Monk Parrot Sleeping in Nest.

Finding A Niche in Publishing Children's Books

Wiggle Room

Nesting on New York City Telephone Pole.

Finch on Bird Feeder.

George and Pip Enjoying Garden with Giant Sunflowers.

Artwork by Bill Young: Illustrationinc.piczo.com
Photography by George P. Sommers.

INSIGHTS FROM AN AUTHOR
Monique Howard on Story
Board and Outlines

As a novice I learned how to write and create picture book outlines by attending workshops. First time writers were instructed to write picture books under a thousand word count. Less is more when creating a picture book. A writer must draw on a large sheet of paper, thirty-two small boxes where sketches will be drawn in each box, making an outline to map out the action scene by scene to help guide the writer in matching the art with the story.

The general rule is for picture books to be thirty- two pages, but sometimes book lengths will vary. Here is a sample of the outline I created for my picture book entitled, **The Moon Creeper**.

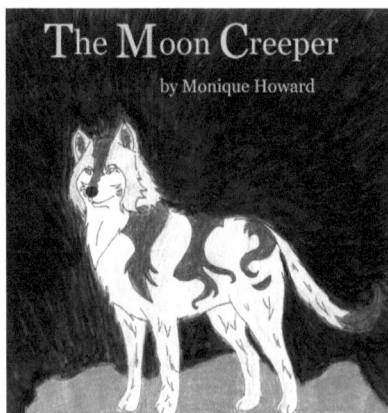

The Moon Creeper, illustrated by Monique Howard

Picture Book Outline

Page one: Moon Creeper looks up at the sky.

Page two: Moon Creeper eats moon rocks.

Page three: A shooting star soars past the moon.

Page four: Moon Creeper leaps into the air and catches the stardust.

Page five: Moon Creeper rubs stardust all over his body.

Page six: Moon Creeper starts to glow and float in the air.

Page seven: Moon Creeper flies.

Page eight: Dust fades. Moon Creeper falls.

Page nine: Moon Creeper lands in a tree and cuts his paw.

Page ten: House lights come on. Girl in pajamas comes outside.

Image of Jia Li from *The Moon Creeper written and illustrated* by Monique Howard

Exchanging Manuscripts

At a workshop I traded stories with other writers. Each member in my group emailed me his or her story. I reviewed each piece of writing, stating the strengths and weaknesses of every manuscript. Going to your local library to pick up books on writing books for children is the key element, which will show a novice what to look for in the genre and age group he or she is hoping to write about. Also, read as many books as you can on your genre of choice.

Learning from master writers will help a great deal. I also searched for a Children's Book publisher on a website called Jacket Flap.

The Writers Market is another good source for hunting down the right publisher. I found Wiggles Press by word of mouth; this small press publisher was recommended to me by an illustrator. Sending out an email or giving someone a call can sometimes be effective.

Bio

Monique Howard – poet, picture book author and middle grade fantasy writer. She is also a freelance illustrator.

Blog: http://author-moniquehoward.blogspot.com

Contact: arthaven.howard73@gmail.com

Wiggle Room

INSIGHTS FROM AN ILLUSTRATOR
Al Margolis on Creating Illustrations

Al Margolis is well-known for his inventive visuals and insightful, humorous illustrations. A Cleveland Art School graduate, his career includes advertising agency art director, and since 2000, owner of Margolis Creative, a graphic design and illustration group.

Al's humorous illustrations have been used in advertising campaigns, children's books and greeting cards. His work has also included advertising for a children's art center, a private school, a foster care and adoption home, and a special needs facility. Helping children enjoy, learn and understand their experiences is an important part of his work. He brings his broad experience and supportive approach to every project.

Input from Al Margolis:
Diagramming and Planning / Book Development
I break the text down to single pages. Then, I diagram the text for ideas and objects that have to be shown on each page. I usually circle them or highlight them in a color.

Many writers prefer working with the words; artists work with visuals. Writers often describe details they would like to see drawn; I prefer to work directly from the text and draw the details described in the story. For me, that's working with the same ideas that the reader will see. They have to match each other when all is said and done.

My practice is to always start with a character development page, present my rough sketches together with the text that will appear on that page and then present the final drawings with the same text for approval - it's a way of working backwards from the final product.

My drawings take about a day each per page, start to finish... including page and document setup. This could take longer if there are more than two main characters.

Maintaining continuity for many characters can be a little time consuming.

Partnering with a Self-Publisher

An ideal author/illustrator relationship is co-ownership. Generally, it can take the illustrator many hours to create the art, including interpretation, design and execution.

The author generally pays for the printing and marketing. The time and money investment seems to be fairly even, if you were to assign an hourly rate to both the writer and the artist.

This can really vary from person to person, and can be argued both ways.

When partnering, the author and illustrator should have a clear contract covering ownership, royalties, sales tracking, and distribution management (shipping of books). It should be a true 50/50 partnership to avoid problems. Key to the success of this relationship is the ability to agree to disagree, and to trust the other's instincts.

The alternative is for the author to own the process, and the artist is hired to illustrate and receives a flat fee.

Creating A Business

Define your goals. If you want the satisfaction of being in print, it's fairly easy to do. You can give or sell books to your immediate circle of friends, charities, neighbors, etc.

You can use on-demand printing, vanity printers, or online albums. There are many ways to print small quantities. If you want to generate bigger sales outside your acquaintances, you have to be sure you start with an idea that has some mass appeal.

Getting the word out can be very time consuming. Some outlets for distribution are libraries, school systems, school classes, giving sample copies to groups, public relations

Finding A Niche in Publishing Children's Books

mailing, social sites, email lists, blogging, book shows, award shows, etc. Holiday postings (Earth Day, Children's Day), boxed sets for gift occasions such as birthdays and graduations, and postings on eBay, craigslist, etc. are other distribution methods.

A one year marketing plan helps; it's the repetition that people often respond to.

Having an interesting "script" about the book when you make your contacts is a plus: why this book would be good and helpful for children to read, etc.

Developing associated items to market helps, too – for example, cups and t-shirts. Business cards help, as well. The business side is another skill set. There is a lot to think about and develop.

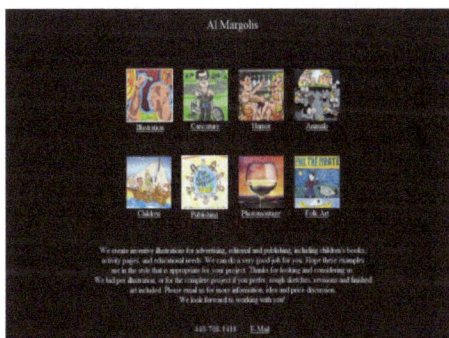

Margolis Creative, Inc.
440-708-1418
565 Mock Orange
Chagrin Falls, OH 44023
ILLUSTRATION:
www.almargolis.com

WiggleRoom

Chapter 4. Process and Procedures

Pricing:

Artists negotiate prices based on time and material costs. It is important to state the following whether the artist sets a price per page or a flat fee for the entire project: when an artist negotiates a price for one flat fee or with a schedule of payments reflecting a deposit and balance timeline, it is important to state what will be delivered and when it is expected.

Normally, a deposit is paid when sketches are received, and the balance is paid upon the receipt of the finished product.

For example: The artist may say, "I can produce sketches in two weeks, but it will take me three months to finish the final art."

The deposit would be due in two weeks, and the balance in three months. However, the book cannot have a publish date in three months.

You must allow time for the edits, reviews, changes, scheduling a proof with the printer, approval and final production.

The average book can take a minimum of two months to produce. If a busy illustrator and productive printer are involved in several projects, it can take up to six months.

The artist should state upfront what revisions will cost and, if additional images are requested, what those additions will cost per page as well.

Deadlines:

Publishers schedule the production of several projects and publications simultaneously; therefore, it is extremely important to have timelines and to meet them.

An artist should consider the time it will take to complete sketches and finishes prior to contracting a project to ensure that the deadlines can be met.

The artist will expect to be paid for work that exceeds the contracted page count, and likewise, the publisher has the right to withhold payment until the artwork is completed.

Be aware of any deadlines because if you cannot meet a deadline, it may require the publisher to hire another artist to redo a project to meet a deadline.

Communicate any delays or request time extensions as soon as you are aware of a need for more time. Affording the publisher this courtesy gives the publisher an opportunity to reschedule printers to reset a publishing date with the authors.

In cases where a book is being submitted for an award or event, delaying the date may impact marketing goals.

For example, I had a book I wanted to release in time for a huge book fair where distributors and agents could purchase the book. When the artist didn't meet

WiiggleRoom

the deadline, I not only had to miss the event, but also missed including it in an award submission. As a result, all the marketing planned for the release of the book fell apart.

Chapter 5. Publishing Elements

Copyright

When writing a story, the author should copyright the work himself with the United States Copyright Office. Copyrights protect the story's content, not its title.

Today copyrights can be applied for online and text files and art can be uploaded via the Internet. Applying online is less expensive than mailing in an original document.

ISBN (International Standard Book Number)

An ISBN is a number that is assigned to your book for tracking sales of your book by your publisher. It is converted into a barcode and placed on the back cover for inventory at bookstores and libraries and for searching a book title on the Internet.

LCCN (Library of Congress Control Number)

An LCCN is assigned by the United States Library of Congress by applying to the Copyright Office and is assigned to books for card catalogs with the Library of Congress.

Only U.S. book publishers are eligible to obtain an LCCN. To receive an LCCN, publishers must list a U.S. place of publication on the title page or copyright page.

Chapter 6. Publishers

Today books are being produced in various ways.

Traditional / Commercial

A Traditional or Commercial Publisher is a large publishing house that accepts submissions directly or through literary agents for publication. They publish large volumes of books.

A traditional publisher can offer an advance to authors in the form of prepaid royalties that are based on projected sales of the book. The author will not receive royalties until the sales of the book exceed the advance payment.

Subsidy Publishers

Subsidy Publishers offer to publish a book for a fee from the author that is used to cover the initial setup cost of producing ISBN, illustrations and prepress setup. These publishers do not offer an advance, but will take income from sales of the book and pay royalties to the author from sales.

Subsidy publishers create marketing materials and venues for helping to promote the book for a small fee or for rights to the book.

They are not considered self-publishing because they have an imprint and ISBN number that is assigned to their company and inventory of books.

Self-publishing

Self-publishing means all development of a book is paid for and managed by the author. Each and every aspect of marketing the book is paid for by the author directly or by a la carte services made available through the self-publishing agent.

The author is involved in purchasing his or her artwork, editing, ISBN, and printing.

The publisher or self-publishing agent simply provides printing services and integration to a web site and sales outlets for the book.

Self-publishing has grown in popularity because of the independence and control authors have over the final product.

However, traditional publishers tend to frown on self-published authors because the product is considered inferior or difficult to market.

With the invention of e-books, iPad, and iPhone, books are reaching readers via several new vehicles. The success of a book is truly determined by the level and quality of the marketing plan that is in place to distribute the book.

Having a well-written and well-illustrated book increases the appeal of the book. But having a great marketing plan and sufficient funds for wide distribution are what will determine sales potential.

Chapter 7. Next Steps

Media coverage and distribution is the name of the game when it comes to sales. Money is the engine that drives the publishing game in the marketplace.

There are several distributors of children's books whose fees to represent a book can range from $100 to $3,000.

Distributors may request an exclusive right to sell your book, and for an agreed upon price, they will present your book to dealers they represent.

Many authors think producing a best seller is automatic.

Actually, to achieve that status, review copies of the book must be in the hands of the media months before the release date of the book. The machine must be well oiled before mainstream coverage occurs.

Traditional publishers will send out a press release and a copy of the book to the review circuit before the book is released. They will do the same with media reviewers and editors during the launch of your book – usually in the first month after release.

Subsidy and self-publishing enterprises may not have the budget for producing (free) review copies or for developing an author's media presence or readership.

Large publishing houses are able to squeeze out the smaller houses because they have the funds to send out review copies and to court the marketplace prior to announcing the release of a book. They also have established relationships with editors that they have built over the years.

Distributors such as Ingram, Baker & Taylor will request a marketing plan for your book prior to agreeing to distribute your book to vendors.

Distributors want to see what the author or publisher plans to do to keep the book moving in the marketplace, especially whether the author plans to attend events, conduct book signings, and utilize promotional channels.

One way distributors keep a book alive is through awards and media coverage.

No publisher - whether traditional, subsidy, or self-publishing - will generate ongoing marketing of a book indefinitely.

If an author truly wants to be taken seriously and to generate sales of their book, it is also their responsibility to keep their name in the media by conducting book signings and readings, and attending events at every opportunity.

If you are promoting your book yourself without a distributor, you can purchase copies of your own book and send them with press releases to the media and sales representatives of a bookstore. You will have taken the first steps toward market visibility.

Authors can purchase media coverage by submitting their books to reviewers who have key relationships with media.

Reviewers charge a fee to write about your book and to forward their articles along to newspapers and media outlets.

It is important to develop a synopsis for the book, print postcards and posters, and create an online presence on websites to help readers discover your book.

The author can also invest in a literary agent to help with a publicity campaign. When deciding to publish a book, one needs to consider the time and effort required to make the book a success for you and the publisher who has agreed to make your book a reality.

Often, the author blames the publisher for the lack of sales when the author did nothing to help with the marketing efforts.

Marketing Plans
Writers are motivated by different goals when planning to write a book:

- Writing to have a career as an author or journalist;
- Writing to record or share experiences and be validated or immortalized;
- Writing as an authority on a topic or field to instruct or educate;
- Writing to offer self-help guidance to inspire others or to target a particular audience, such as children.

Wiggle Room

Publishers are looking for good books by authors who are considering writing as a career, whether they have one book to sell or plan to pen several books in the future.

Not everyone wants to pursue a writing career. A publisher may be able to deduce this and decide to reject an author because the story is too personal or shows a lack of experience or dedication to writing.

The publisher may fear that after they invest in the book, the author will expend little effort to sell to anyone other than a few friends or family members. In that case, the book will not be profitable for the publisher.

As a professional writer, you will need some plan of action for gaining visibility and building some public relations around your new book and yourself.

Here are some key elements to include in your marketing plan:

- *Brand* – choose the brand of your company and determine what sets you apart
- *Internet* – develop websites, blogging sites, and online communities
- *Synopsis* – write a brief description of the story's theme, climates, and characters. Include release date, publisher, book cover, and contact information
- *Press Release* – the press release announces the book's launch, an appearance by the author at a book signing, or an event where an author will be

speaking or headlining. Include your synopsis in your release

- *Public Relations* – distribute news of your book through news wires, an agent, and by hosting events such as book signings, release parties, and speaking engagements
- *Marketing Materials* – order bookmarks, postcards, business cards and other items you would like to use to promote your book. At events you may want to give out t-shirts, magnets, or posters featuring your book cover
- *Publicity Plan* – develop a list of bookstores, literary conferences or book fairs and launch your own parties and readings
- *Awards* – research award programs where the book can be submitted for consideration
- *Multimedia Presentation* – consider YouTube, DVDs, CDs, email blast and other technologies for presenting your book or announcing publishing events.

Brand

Brand is a company's identity that positions it in the marketplace. Think McDonalds. All of its products reinforce the same image. Professional speakers and public personalities invest money in developing their brand of speech and appearance to be recognized in the media and by the public.

By the same token, for an individual author, your brand is your identity. You become known by the topics you cover in your stories, your style of writing, the kind of illustrations you use and your personality or presentation.

Finding A Niche in Publishing Children's Books

WiggleRoom

As an author of children's books making personal appearances, you must consider how parents and children will relate to your personality. Are you fun, friendly, and approachable?

What props can you use or jokes can you share that will help kids relate to you? You will need an understanding of age-appropriate topics as well as patience if you ask for questions and feedback.

Media Kit
Authors must develop a media kit for packaging and presenting their book. The kit should include a headshot, postcard with a book cover, a press release and a synopsis.

Include review copies for editors, buyers, and bookstores you want to stock your book. Producing and sending DVDs / CDs may be less expensive, especially if you can burn them at home. However, most people want to see the finished product: autograph the copy, especially if it's a limited edition.

Synopsis
A publisher or editor can help you develop a brief, well written description of the book.

Be sure to describe key characters, present the theme and tell the conclusion of the story. A synopsis is not a teaser to pitch a story.

The story is already written and editors don't have time to guess how the story ends. A synopsis will be a determining factor in the placement of your book: for example, will it be in the mystery section or is it a picture book? Include page length, target audience,

release date, publisher, book cover and contact information.

Press Release
A synopsis can be the bones of your release; however, the release should announce the - who, what, when, and where of the release date, an event such as a book signing, or an appearance where you are speaking or headlining.

Send press releases to local newspapers to the attention of the Editor covering children's books.

Public Relations
Determine how you will distribute news about your book: select newswires, an agent, and host events such as book signings, release parties, and speaking engagements.

Consider uploading media news to free newswires or *The Associate Press* or their affiliates directly.

Here are few sources to consider (there are thousands more on the Internet).

http://www.i-newswire.com
http://www.newswiretoday.com
http://www.optaros.com/blogs/free-alternatives-pr-newswires
http://hosted.ap.org/specials/bluepage.html#ma
http://www.ap.org

Marketing Materials
Decide how much money you will budget to launch or announce your new book and what tools will help you get noticed at events - bookmarks, postcards, business cards, t-shirts, magnets, and posters featuring

your book cover – even placing an ad in a magazine or online. Consider the cost carefully.

Publicity Plan

List the bookstores, literary conferences, book fairs, and/or launch parties where you want to distribute your book, as well as where you want to give readings. Then calculate the quantity of media kits or marketing materials you will need to mail and give away during those events.

Draft a budget for the cost of travel to and from book fairs, and for the registration costs for attending events. Publishers tend to be involved in national or international events and leave the planning of the local circuit and small community events to the author. Publishers will offer bestselling authors the luxury of covering expenses. However, for new authors, subsidy and self-publishing agents and even small publishers will expect you to split or cover your own expenses.

Think of it like this: the sales teams go to tradeshows, not the office secretary or customer service reps. It's the sales teams that bring in the clients, and that's their job. As an author, it's your job to sell – welcome to the sales team.

If you bring in sales, you bring dollars to a company, which can be used to cover expenses.

A great salesperson will be at all the trade shows. Someone who goes to have fun and spends money and never lands a client may not be attending the next trade show.

A publisher may fund your attendance at one or two events but if there are no sales results, they will seek another author on their team who will attract a crowd and bring in the dollars.

If you can host or attend an event that draws a paying crowd, your publisher will notice.

Internet
An Internet site is a great way to build your brand but it won't bring sales unless you drive them there. The same is true of blogs.

Blogs like FaceBook, Ning, and Twitter or a custom designed one in your brand may keep your costs down, but blogs take up valuable personal time to maintain. You can schedule a time when you will be online and even post it to the page.

Let bloggers know when you will be live online (e.g., Tuesday and Thursdays at 3 PM) to respond to their messages so they do not expect you to be available 24/7. Or you may want to join a website that will send you an email when people have signed on so you can be available.

Twitter, Facebook and Ning will update you via email about postings and activity online.

You should notify your publisher of any events and web pages you have developed – even if you maintain yours yourself - because some readers will inquire about you directly to your publisher. If the publisher doesn't know about your activities, they cannot tell your readers or the media.

WiggleRoom

Managing your own blog or website, in addition to your listing on your agent's website, is often best because you can update it yourself with news without waiting until your publishing team has time to post.

Awards

Make a list of award programs that target your book's format and topic. List the deadlines and what must be included with submissions. Determine if only the publisher can submit (often the case). Then, send the list to your publisher to see if they will submit for you. You can ask them to complete the form in exchange for you covering the submission fee.

Reviews

List the names of editors who review books or of professional book reviewers and send them a complimentary copy of your book with any promotional materials. Some professional book reviewers charge a fee and some publish online or in newsletters.

Budget

Whether you have a marketing plan with one or two events or a list of ten, you must have the time in your schedule to execute this plan. You must also have the necessary funds.

Listing the cost for events, materials and mailings on a spreadsheet will help you decide how much you can afford.

You must know whether to start slow or if you can hire an agent to work for you for a commission.

The next page has a mock budget that shows that an author needs to sell 450 copies of his own book at two events to break even on the marketing plan. Sales that exceed 900 copies will begin to bring a profit to the author.

Table 1.<u>An Aggressive Plan for Visibility</u>

Budget	Frequency /QTY	Cost	Total
Internet – Monthly Charges	12	15	27
Synopsis – Cost / Fee	3	250	750
Press Release	3	250	750
Marketing Materials			
Postcards	1	100	100
Bookmarks	1	100	100
T-Shirts	1	500	500
Events			
BEA*	1	250	250
ALA**	1	250	250
Community Fair	5	100	500
Awards			0
IPB***	1	80	80
Travel			0
NYC/Airfare	1	200	200
D.C./ Airfare	1	200	200
Accommodations			0
NYC/Hotel	1	500	500
D.C./ Hotel	<u>1</u>	<u>250</u>	<u>250</u>
			$4,457.00
Sales 50% Author Rate ($5.47)	Breakeven		813
Books			
Books for NY 200	450	5.47	$2,461.50
Books for DC 100	450	5.47	<u>$2,461.50</u>
			$4,923.00

Finding A Niche in Publishing Children's Books

WiggleRoom

*Book Expo America – http://www.bookexpoamerica.com
**American Library Association – http://www.ala.org.
***Independent Book Publisher Association –
http://www.ibpaonline.org/pubresources/events.aspx

WiiggleRoom

INSIGHTS FROM AN AUTHOR
JEAN SMITH ANDREWS: My Path to Publishing

I started writing seriously when my first child was only a toddler. I recall reading to him daily, but African-American children's books were a rarity. During bath time and naptime, I found myself creating stories that shortly were mailed to well-known publishers.

Rejection after rejection halted my writing for children, but led to other writings and publications. Among my accomplishments are two essays, and a chapter for a book. I've written a play and a life balancing workshop/workbook, and have a novel in progress. Still, the passion for writing children's books burned within, thus becoming my solace while undergoing many of life's transitions, resulting in ten unpublished children's books.

After moving to Charlotte nearly four years ago, I got the bug again. ***There's No Mouse in My New House*** needed a publisher. Subsequently, I began debating...do I self-publish or go with AuthorHouse, Xlibris, or one of the others? Without an illustrator for my book, I had the option to utilize one of theirs.

However, while attending an authors/illustrators conference I heard repeatedly, "You will not have any control over the changes of your manuscript or the illustrations." No control of my situation, not me!

Finally, an African-American Writers Conference was being held in Charlotte but unfortunately I had plans to be out of town. When I returned I located the website and a list of illustrators that led me to Berry Holly, the illustrator of my first book, which is being published by Wiggles. I arranged a meeting with Berry

Finding A Niche in Publishing Children's Books

to review his portfolio. Appreciating his artistic gift, we entered into a contractual agreement to work together until that book found a publisher. Now I had a story and an illustrator.

Berry recommended I contact his publisher and I did. However, I knew almost immediately that this individual was not properly conducting her business, so I dismissed any affiliations.

Disappointed again, I joined various organizations that provided great opportunities for networking and it was an artist who shared information about a local publishing company. I was thrilled and quickly made contact.

Within two weeks I had an appointment with the CEO and discovered a professional operation with more than 10 years experience and over fifty accomplished authors. The children's books that were scattered on the table said, "Yes, this is it." My manuscript was accepted, a contract written and then came the disappointment. It would cost me $1,400 to subsidize the publisher's cost. I was already paying the illustrator with whom I shared my frustration. He told me of an advertisement on Craigslist soliciting new authors and illustrators and suggested I make a call.

Wiggles Press to the rescue! I contacted Rochelle Thorpe and the relationship began. However, as with any relationship, there was that occasional tug of war. She was fairly new to the business and I was also a novice. She needed control and I wanted control. I was being critical as I edited her website. Then I realized, she was just moving too fast so I offered her advice. My motherly instinct pervaded. We were both

---

Finding A Niche in Publishing Children's Books

out-spoken but knew when to retreat and come back with different perspectives. I now await the release of my first published children's book and am now inspired to follow up with a second, third…and will get back to the novel.

Rochelle challenged me, inspired me, set me off, released me from my contract, allowed me to come back and loved me for the person I am. At times we were both wishy-washy but this has been a valuable experience.

During the process of being published with Wiggles, I learned:

- While I had my own illustrator, I shouldn't expect the publisher to agree with my choice.
- The author should have a plan.
- Keep your emotions in check and try your best to be objective.
- Give precise instructions to the illustrator; character sketch, time of year, and type of art…pastels, oils, etc. Preferences of bold, subdued, or mix. Have that conversation often to minimize surprises!
- Convey to the publisher through well-thought out emails. Don't waste their time rambling.
- Don't make hasty decisions. Allow a day or two to ponder over revised manuscripts. I must have ten versions of **There's No Mouse**…Maintain an updated file and delete the dysfunctional ones.
- Sometimes the original story is "the best" and we should be careful of over-working it.
- If the publisher says your book will be better as a soft cover and you want hardback, then maybe you can negotiate if you are willing to invest in the printing. When contracting your

own illustrator be clear whom he/she should be sending the artwork to.

- Visit the library and ideas about types of illustrations, layout, and even word fonts.
- Study book covers to help in determining if you want yours to be bold and daring. Don't be afraid to take risk.
- Put your ego in the drawer!

My greatest challenge now is to market myself. Drafts for press releases for my hometown newspaper and alumni associations have been drafted. Additionally, I have notified organizations that I am affiliated with, met with the owner of a bookstore and French bakery about holding book signings, and contacted the local library. I am researching literary events in the area and plan to contact some churches.

My email contacts are being updated using business cards that I've collected. I'm not a fan of Facebook but will consider signing on. I plan to visit barbershops, beauty salons and any place that I can find a mom or dad. In the fall I plan to contact the elementary schools, local "Y" and After-School program. I will be very busy.

I've asked my son, a graphic artist, to create my new business card that reads, Jean Smith Andrews, Children's author. Although my life has taken me around corners that led to some dead ends, I've reached another goal at age 67. Hooray!

Chapter 8. Review Team

As a new author it is important to join a writing association or select a group of friends and family who will help you review the copy, contract, and illustrations.

Obtaining feedback from others is valuable in this process. It is important to make sure these individuals have a writing background or have a literary interest.

Often the advice given to an author can vary because not everyone knows the industry or the objectives you want to reach.

A bookclub may also be useful in reviewing a book. Librarians and teachers in school may be willing to engage a classroom in reviewing a new book.

Having a dependable review team is *key* to helping authors develop an audience for the book as well.

Unfortunately, as a publisher I have also experienced the nightmares of too many cooks in the kitchen.

An author's indecisiveness can also stem from poor advice they are given by friends and family and can be the demise of a project as well as a good relationship with your publisher.

A new and promising author terminated a publishing agreement within months of publishing because she thought her book would be a bestseller and make money simply because it was online at major Internet sites.

Wiggle Room

However, the book had no sales. Populating the Internet with a book's title and cover does not guarantee that a book will sell.

Publishers, like authors, are dependent on online distributors to report sales and revenue. These distributors receive a 40% to 70% discount from the list price of a book.

Sometimes a distributor does not report sales accurately or pay the publisher for sales made through their channels. Then the publisher has no income and cannot pay royalties to their authors.

The only dependable sales a publisher has are those made through their direct channels via the publisher's website, or through purchases made directly from a bookstore or distributors.

Publishers can track the number of books being printed and shipped to a distributor with whom they have contracted.

Online and on demand vendors are third party vendors and a huge level of blind trust exists with these sales channels because the volume of printing is unknown to the publisher or author for that matter.

Both the author and publisher rely on online channels to report sales and pay royalties, but it's a risk.

Chapter 9. Authors: Your Publisher is Your Best Friend

As a writer, you want to keep in mind that your publisher is making your dream of producing a book come true. As a result, gaining the trust and respect of the publisher is very important.

Publishers are utilizing their funds, contacts and resources on your behalf; until you are generating revenues from book sales, you are a liability.

Remember that publishers are human too, and have limits on how much demand they can absorb. Traditional publishers limit the number of books they publish based on how many people they can manage.

Publishers offer advances or extended contracts based on how positive their relationship is with an author but also on how much effort an author has expended toward promoting sales of the book.

In fact, a publisher often decides whether to keep or drop a title based on what an author has contributed to generating sales. Even authors that publishers find difficult to work with are often retained because they generate sales that are vital to the publisher's bottom line.

Being signed by a big publisher is exciting. The number of people assigned to manage your book will vary; however, they are all on the same publishing house team. If you are deemed difficult to work with by any one member, your relationship with the whole company will be affected.

If you are working with a small publisher with limited resources, maintaining this positive relationship is even more important. If an author makes demands that exceed the capacity of a small publisher or that jeopardize their reputation, the publisher is more than likely going to drop the project to minimize their liability.

When you are earning thousands or millions of dollars for a publisher, you can make more demands on that enterprise; until then, the interdependency of the relationship is key to both the author's and publisher's success and reputation.

Keeping your publisher happy and generating sales are both key components of a successful relationship between author and publisher. You might be tolerated as a diva if your sales are through the roof; your behavior will be like the elephant in the room that nobody talks about. However, if you behave like a diva and your book is not selling, a publisher will escort you to the exit faster than you can blink!

Chapter 10.   Royalties

Royalties are a percentage of sales or commission paid to authors and illustrators based on the sales of their books.

An advance is a set amount paid in anticipation of sales of a book. The publisher projects what they will earn from your book and then pays an advance on that projection.

If projected sales goals are exceeded, then additional royalties are likely to be paid and new book deals extended to the author.

If the projected sales goals are not met, you can expect that your book may be dropped from syndication and future submissions rejected.

Although advances are given, no royalties are paid until the revenues from sales match the advance already paid. After the advance is repaid, then and only then will royalties be paid to the author from subsequent sales.

Subsidy and self-publishers may not pay an advance to a new writer but may pay royalties reflecting a percentage of sales from a book as soon as the book is printed and sold.

Normally these royalties are 10% to 40% of the list price of a book. *List Price* is the same as the *Retail Price* of a book.

Most books are sold through distributors who receive discounts of 40% to 50 % off the list price.

Wiggle Room

Because the publisher has already discounted the book to the distributor, royalties then paid to the author represent 5% to 15% of sales.

Authors make the mistake of thinking that their book, which may have a list price of $20 and has sold 1,000 copies, has generated $20,000 in income for the publisher and therefore, they should have a $4,000 check coming.

In actuality, 1,000 books sold via bookstores and distributors only earned the publisher between $8,000 and $10,000 because the distributors and bookstores received a 40% to 50% discount off the list price.

Then, the publisher has to deduct production costs from that $8,000 to $10,000.

If the printing cost $5,000, then the publisher's gross profit is only $3,000 to $5,000.

Now, if the publisher has agreed to pay you a 20% royalty, then the publisher owes you between $600 and $1,000, leaving the publisher with a net profit of $2,400 to $4,000 from the sales of 1,000 copies of your book.

Keep in mind that if income from sales of your book doesn't exceed the publisher's investment in printing, illustrators, and marketing efforts, the publisher suffers a loss. This is why publishers set a goal of selling 1,000 or more copies of a book to ensure that they at least recoup their costs.

My success as a publisher is determined by the volume of books sales my authors produce. If a book takes off and sells extremely well, that success will

have an impact on the reputation and respect Wiggles Press gains in the media and publishing industry.

Retail Sales:
Book sells for $20.00

This means the list price or retail price is $20.00.

The royalty to the author is 20% means the author earns a $4 royalty.

Distribution Sales:
$20.00 – 40% discount = $12

The royalty earned on distribution sales is 10%. The author earns $1.20 as a royalty.

The publisher has to deduct production cost / per unit cost from the retail or list price of a book to earn a profit.

The price of a book is determined by the per unit production cost plus the discount given to the distributor added to the royalties.

In other words, the cost of printing, illustrating, and overhead has to be reflected by the price for the publisher to break even.

For example:

List Price Sale ($20) - print cost ($5) - Royalty ($4) = $11. The publisher has $11 to use for production cost (illustrators, design, editing and marketing) and what remains is the net revenue generated.

Wiggle Room

At the Distributor Price ($12) - print ($5) - royalty ($1.20) = $5.80

The publisher has $5.80 to use for production cost (illustrators, design, editing and marketing) and what remains is the net revenue generated.

WiggleRoom

Chapter 11.   Costs

The average cost incurred for each published book is as follows.

1) *Illustrations* - $500 to $1,000 for illustrations depending on the number of illustrations and artist agreement.
2) *Editing* - $50 to $300 for editing copy depending on how much editing is needed and the page count.
3) *Graphic Design* - $100 per hour for 8 to 20 hours, or $800 to $2,000, per book for graphic design and layout of the book depending on the number of pages, illustrations and rounds of pre-press preparation (setup and edits).
4) *Proof Production* - $20 to $100 plus normal shipping for proofs; add $50 for rush orders when deadlines are shortened to meet a specific date ($60 for hardcover proofs).
5) *Printing* - $3 to $8/book depending on color and quantity.
6) *Author Copies* - 50% of list price plus shipping for ten free author copies.
7) *Copyright* - $35 for online ordering of Copyrights and a Library of Congress Control Number (free to publishers only. Some vendors charge for LCCNs).
8) *ISBN and Barcodes* - $50 to $75 each, bulk sold to publishers at $500 for 100 ISBNs – barcodes are additional.
9) *Web Hosting* - $200 for Web Host depending on functionality (ecommerce sites are more) - web content, design and hosting. Editing content and design is usually $100 per hour / 2 hour minimum.

WiggleRoom

10) *Media Writing* - $250/$125 each for synopsis and press release.
11) Collateral – $250 for design and printing 100-200 postcards and/or bookmarks.

The investment in production costs for publishing 1,000 copies of a book using mid-range numbers is as follows:

$ 750 Illustrations (16 for a 32 page book)
$ 175 Editing (2.5 hours at $50 per hour)
$1,600 Graphic Design (16 hours)
$ 60 10 free copies + shipping (paperback)
$ 20 Proofs
$5,289 Printing
$ 35 Copyright and LCCN
$ 10 ISBN & Barcodes
$ 150 Web Page design / hosting fee
$ 125 Synopsis
$ 125 Press Release
$ 150 Post Cards

= $8,489 Total Costs

WiggleRoom

Chapter 12.   Printing & Pricing

Print Quality and Selecting a Printer in the United States Versus Overseas Off-Shore Printers.

The quality of a book is determined by materials used and coloration.

Printers bid for projects with clients who submit a Request of Quote (RFQ). The RFQ should include a description of the book's specifications:

1. Book cover size in width by height dimensions (8x10, 6x9, 5x7, 7x10, 9x6, etc.).
2. Paper weight (60, 80, 100 lb or board book).
3. Binding type (perfect bound, stapled or saddle stitch, or coil / spiral bound – plastic or metal). Page count will determine the type of binding that can be applied to a book.

Most printers are happy to send samples of paper and binding to clients. Otherwise, you can request samples to review on site at their facility.

Some printers outsource cover finishes like UV coating, foil, and embossing, as well as the production of hard covers and the binding of the finished book. Therefore, it is very important to know your printer's capabilities.

When outsourcing is involved, then costs may be higher and production slower because the process passes through several hands and each must be paid.

The more production is concentrated onsite at one facility, the higher the savings.

Print brokers can take your specifications and shop around to a number of printers to find the best price; however, that price will include the broker's fee for managing the production with the printer, and for travel costs and delivery.

Experienced brokers know who does what, where, when, why, and how and can be useful in a crunch. Brokers may also carry samples of work done by printers and production houses; however, you should request paper samples to review to be sure your expectations will be met.

Printers in the United States have higher costs than overseas production houses. However, it is very difficult to know the quality of overseas printing agents without having the time to have samples sent to you, unless they have been referred by a reliable source.

Also, when hiring an overseas team, you must monitor shipping costs and timelines closely to stay within budget.

A printer in China may ship by boat and not by air, so it can be three to six months to receive a shipment of 1,000 books or more. Even if it cost you only $1 per book, if you don't have the time, don't spend the money.

Some American printers are very reliable and cost-effective too. Either way, the quantity of books printed will determine the unit cost for any production. The higher the quantity, the lower the unit cost.

Printing 50 books costs twice as much as printing 100, and likewise, 100 cost three times as much as printing 1,000. However, if you don't have $3,000 to $5,000 to print 1,000 copies and your distribution channels are not in place to generate sales of 1,000 copies, you are better served printing a small amount and developing successful distribution channels that demand more sales.

You can take the revenues from the sales of your first batch and reinvest in printing larger quantities on a second production. Besides, printing too many on a first run and being left with hundreds of books collecting dust is not cost-effective in the long run and forces you to discount a book to make it sell.

If you have the space for storing inventory, then this may be a risk you're willing to take. However, if you don't have the storage capacity, then it is best to grow the sales demand before ordering huge quantities of books.

As a publisher, I would rather build a sense of demand and intrigue by saying that a book has sold out and is on reorder than pick up the phone to call a discount dealer to beg him to take books off my hands after three months of marketing efforts or clean out inventory with a two-for-one special.

Pricing a Book
Common sense says to price books to fit the marketplace demand.

Wiggle Room

If publishers are selling 8 x10 covers with 32 pages of text and illustrations for $6.99 to $10.95, your price should be within that range.

Determining pricing is the same as with any other product:

ROI = [(Payback - Investment)/Investment)]*100
As stated before, publishers will be interested in (Price x Quantity) – (Production cost).

Budgeting

Assess the costs of printing and illustrations, royalties, and marketing expenses incurred to produce the book to determine your breakeven point.

Here is an example for 1,000 books if a book is priced at $19.95 and is sold directly at full price:

$5,289.89	Printing cost 1,000 books ($5.29/book)
$1,600.00	Graphic Design
$1,000.00	Illustrator fee ($1.00/book)
$ 255.00	Editing/Proofs/Author Copies
$3,990.00	Author royalties (20% of retail price)
$ 997.50	Artist royalties 5% of retail price)
$ 655.00	Marketing/Collateral Expenses
$13,787.39	Total production cost for 1,000 books

How many books must sell to break even?

$13,787.39/$19.95 = 691 books.

However, in the publishing world, books are sold at discount. Amazon and some other wholesalers require discounts of up to 60% to 70% of the list price on books to cover their expenses; this makes the publisher's share even smaller. Due to rising costs, many publishers are offsetting their losses by limiting the number of authors they take on and by expanding the channels their books can sell through – like electronic formats for e-books, Internet downloads and iPad applications.

These new formats are cheaper than printing and can increase sales volume without increasing production cost.

Here is an example for 1,000 books with a retail price of $19.95, discounted 40% ($11.97):

$5,289.89	Printing cost 1,000 books ($5.29/book)
$1,600.00	Graphic Design
$1,000.00	Illustrator fee ($1.00/book)
$ 255.00	Editing/Proofs/Author Copies
$1,995.00	Author royalties (10% of retail price)
$ 997.50	Artist royalties 5% of retail price)
$ 655.00	Marketing/Collateral Expenses
$11,792.39	Total production cost for 1,000 books

How many books must sell to break even?

$11,792.39/$11.97 = 985 books

Marketing expenses may include other factors like commissions on sales by distributors, cost of posters and postcards created to promote a book and deductions given on sales through various channels.

Publishers are not obligated to share their production costs with authors, but they will communicate their sales goals for the book. Authors can calculate an estimate of cost by dividing the sales goals by the quantity of books produced.

Distributors

Know who your distributors are – it is horrible to choose a distributor who will discount your books during the first year of sales and not allow you to earn your list price before they begin listing it online at one-half your retail price.

Such book dealers will not pay you a decent commission as a result. One such dealer I had even deducted the shipping cost of returning unsold books that they failed to pay royalties on after selling several copies. I had little to nothing left for covering author royalties.

Bookstores

Know your bookstores, too. Obviously, it is important to determine whether the bookstore is successful or in financial trouble.

Many are willing to take new authors on consignment.

Bookstores can wait until the end of the year, or until the last possible moment, to pay for books sold on consignment. If they are going out of business, you may not be paid at all.

Be prepared to hire a collection agency to chase your accounts payable, and send invoices often. To help the bookstore sell for you, it is important to host a book signing or to attract traffic to the store by listing them in the marketing materials.

Call the bookstore periodically to see if the book is selling and when you can expect payment for sales.

WiiggleRoom

Ask distributors and bookstores not to discount your book until after six months, or for a predetermined term of service.

Your list price is locked in so you can maximize your earnings for a set period of time.

If you must discount your book, the best time is during holidays or promotional events or campaigns. If the price then goes back up, then it was a true special. If it is discounted and stays discounted, it is a clearance sale.

It is best to check references of distributors and to join the Independent Book Sellers Association to meet bookstore owners who are willing to support your growth. Your sales and pricing strategy should enable them to make a living.

Be willing to provide materials and help with marketing at any book signings and events they host. The relationship should be mutually supportive, especially if the store is struggling financially. You can help attract traffic to a store that has supported your book in the past.

INSIGHTS ON WORKING WITH PRINT BROKERS

CEO of NexGraphix, Terryl Calloway has been an acquaintance of mine since college. When I started my career in marketing again I was eager to utilize the services of a friend and while publishing my first book, he was the first one to support me by finding a great price for printing my book.

In turn as I had more leverage in my role as a Marketing Director I sought opportunities to contract

WiggleRoom

his services for business at the corporate level. Opportunities for small business and especially minority-owned operations in the printing world are scarce because it is believed the work will not be of commercial quality or deadlines and capacity for jobs requiring thousands of units cannot be well executed.

One such experience that mirrored that assumption was landing a small job for a one-piece display card.

The fee for the job was only $1,000, which was miniscule compared to the work being brokered out to firms equal to the size of this firm but owned by non-minority businesses. Yet this simple project was micro-managed because of the lack of confidence in a minority-owned company.

As a print procurement specialist for a large retail operation in the sportswear industry, I came to realize that there was no policing of diversity initiatives to insure that minority-owned businesses were offered a chance to respond to a Request For Proposal/Quote (RFP/RFQ).

Most brokers were eager to land an RFQ and quickly responded to inquires. Many offered samples of their work and agreed to meet with you to review specs for projects.

Large or small printers are able to tell you what their client can provide and confirm turnaround times or constraints.

Brokers are a great asset when you don't have a direct relationship with a printer or only have a few projects to produce.

Landing deals can be a rough road for minority-owned businesses in the printing field whether you are a supplier or a broker.

The diversity initiative was a well-articulated business objective seldom practiced.

With thousands invested in printing equipment licenses and only community-based clients as a revenue stream, Terryl had the wisdom to restructure his operation from a production house to a brokerage agency.

As a broker he could hand off projects to print facilities that could indeed match commercial marketing demands while affording him the opportunity of building a large clientele through expanding his business relations.

In building relationships, Terryl could gain the confidence of key players who might bring lucrative contracts his way.

As a publisher I still have a reliable friend and viable colleague to turn to for printing books and materials.

Conclusion: Finding My Niche in Publishing Children's Books

As a child, I wrote poems, and later, as a teenage traveler, I began to keep journals of my experiences living abroad in Asia. After graduating from college, I landed my first job as an Administrative Assistant to the Public Relations Manager for Monitor Radio, a broadcast service of The Christian Science Monitor.

In this role I developed media kits and wrote copy for developing press releases and bios of on-air personalities for marketing to outlets for syndication.

In my late 30s, I married a news reporter who wrote for a community newspaper, Boston's Bay State Banner, and freelanced for the Boston Globe for over 20 years. In observing him, I began to understand the distinction between a writer and a reporter. A reporter goes after a story about events occurring in people's lives or newsworthy events.

A creative writer or a journalist writes because they have a story to tell and a passion to share their insights through prose or poetry.

The reporter reports the news, while the writer creates the story that becomes the news.

In 2002, I began composing my first book, **The Majestic Crane**, from my collection of journals about my travels to Asia as a young African-American exchange student studying Chinese.

I solicited illustrators for the book and was shocked when the world-renowned Japanese Master Artist Kaji Aso agreed to illustrate the book.

As I fondly recall visiting him in his home with a box of photos of my family and travels to help him create artwork for the book, I remember that I gave Kaji little guidance. He intuitively knew exactly what images related to each chapter and generated illustrations that captured each chapter's theme.

Soon, the book was completed and I self-published my very first book.

At the time, I had only submitted the book to a handful of publishers. Since I had little success, I decided to move ahead on my own.

Not many African-Americans have had similar experiences to my own, as I was the first student of color to participate in a Chinese Exchange Program in Taiwan prior to 1981. I wanted to make sure my story was told from an authentic perspective.

Fortunately for me, my husband Richard had traveled to China with me in 2002 and was a catalyst for me to complete my book. He co-authored chapters related to our time together teaching in Hei Long Jiang, China's Northeast Province, and he helped to edit the book.

When Richard passed away from complications related to treatment for his leukemia, I soon found writing therapeutic for healing my broken heart, just as it had been while I was going through a difficult divorce before we married.

Finding A Niche in Publishing Children's Books

This time, I filled journals with feelings and experiences we shared raising our children (his stepchildren) Nathaniel and Misha, as well as experiences raising our newborn son, Gabriel. I continued to write about experiencing his passing and mothering solo.

These journals became new book; **Captain Remarkable: Girls Can Be Superheroes Too!** and **The Adventures of Gabe** that includes the stories **Gabe and the Park and His Big Toy Box, Gabe and the Bike, Gabe's Nantucket Adventure**, and **Gabe and Storybooks.**

In 2008, I met with a friend who was excited about a book he had drafted. He pulled out a copy of illustrated pages filled with poems he had written.

The book was bound with plastic coil and although beautiful, not in a format for selling a book for profit. As I perused the copy, I was thrilled to read the poetry, and the beautiful illustrations were truly outstanding. I left our meeting that day with a commitment to find him a publisher for his book.

This author was the renowned civil rights activist and educator Mel King. When I got home I searched the Internet to find a publisher who would consider his book.

This is how I came across a listing for an African-American subsidy publisher, Dyahnne Terrell-Alston of Sweeties Books. After a brief telephone conversation, I was sent a contract for Mel King's book and presented the contract to Mel for consideration.

He followed up with a telephone call to the publisher and proceeded with the contract.

Once the contract was signed and funds sent, an electronic proof of the book was sent to us for approval. However, the deadline for delivering the books was not met.

The publisher promised to deliver books in time for a book signing. I had booked a signing at a local bookstore and we proceeded as planned to host the event.

On the day of the signing, no books had arrived. The bookstore owner and I were at a loss, but Mel King graciously conducted a review of his book using a PowerPoint presentation. He read samples of poetry from his personal prototype of the book.

The bookstore took orders, which we were able to fill once the books finally arrived.

As a literary agent for the book, **Streets: Poem Book**, I learned lesson one the hard way: never host or plan an event prior to having a book in hand. It was a hard lesson to learn because I was caught in the middle between a publisher who didn't deliver on time and a disappointed author. My reputation was on the line with people I valued.

Worst of all, the publisher's broken promises strained the relationship between my client and me. When Mel King had future events, he would thank everyone involved with his book. He would thank the artist and those who were part of his editorial team, but never was my role as his agent ever mentioned.
Frustrated and hurt that my reputation was damaged by an unreliable third party, I almost crumbled with

despair at disappointing someone whom I greatly admired.

During this time, I was approached by a recruiter to work at Converse Incorporation as a print procurement specialist. I spent several months brokering contracts with printers for the development of catalogs, retail books and promotional materials for the famous sportswear and apparel enterprise (Nike subsidy).

Within months, an author of children's books approached me to help her publish her book, which was already written, designed and formatted for publishing. She only needed an agent. When I learned she was experiencing as many difficulties with Sweeties as Mel King had experienced, I decided I had to do something to remedy these situations.

This is when I began to research how to obtain ISBN numbers and what it took to become a publisher. I realized that my new job was teaching me how to negotiate print brokering and it taught me how to present bids to printers – describing the specifications for a print production.

That's when I realized I could combine this experience with my previous experiences as a marketing director to begin publishing books on my own terms.

As a marketing director, I had created marketing materials and websites, as well as conducted trade show and media events. I had also recently earned a Master of Arts in Integrated Marketing from Emerson College, where I refined my ability to create branding, develop product marketing, and manage relationships with the media.

It seemed I was fully equipped with the experiences I needed to launch a small publishing house. To get started, I contracted with a few artists to begin developing illustrations for my first set of books. I submitted RFQs (Requests for Quotes) to printers to get pricing for publishing my books, and I was writing and rewriting business plans for starting Wiggles Press as a DBA. I planned to incorporate once I had a track record for a raising capital.

Just when I was ready to print the books, Converse announced layoffs and I was forced to postpone my publishing ambitions. I was balancing caring for my family as a recent widow and trying to pay the illustrators with whom I had contracted. Everyone was demanding payment. Soon everyone was frustrated and angry with my delay or nonpayment. What was I to do? I applied for unemployment to keep moving ahead.

Having only worked for six months at Converse, I only got 11 weeks of unemployment benefits. Shortly after New Years, 2009, my funds ran dry.

One artist settled for ½ of the contracted price for her illustrations and granted me the right to publish the book we started together. However, the other artist filed suit against me for full payment for a book that never saw the light of day.

This is when Mel King sent me a true sign of forgiveness and friendship when he sent a new writer my way to publish (Robert Peters). When I met with Robert Peters, I was more than eager to prove myself.

Finding A Niche in Publishing Children's Books

Robert wanted to use his savings to create a book that would earn him income.

I created a budget, marketing plan, and researched distribution channels for marketing his book. Likewise Robert, his family and friends championed his efforts to be a success by lining up several events for book signing and reading opportunities.

Our publishing contract stated that royalties would not be generated. As a result, I would be a publishing agent versus a full-fledged publisher. In other words, I would be the publisher and promoter for a flat fee. Accepting a flat fee without revenues from royalties limited what I could do for the author.

Without earning a commission for sales, there would be a very small budget of executing full-fledged marketing and promotions.

Again, I was left with almost no funds to pay for marketing materials or for developing distribution channels. Distributors require a fee for placing a book in their sales channels and a 15 % commission on sales they make.

The publisher can earn as little as 20% from sales of a book that they have sold at a 40% to 70% discount to distributors. And when the publisher has to pay a royalty out of the 30% of sales that is left, there is very little return until revenues from sales increase beyond the production cost.

Robert did not want to spend money on distributors or discount his books. Against my advice, he wanted to generate direct sales from events to make his full list price.

Six months later, a buyer from Barnes & Noble called and indicated they wanted to carry the book but it had to be with one of their distribution agents. This provided the proof I needed that I had given him the correct advice, but by then his budget for moving forward with the distributor had been exhausted.

I explained to Robert that libraries and bookstores will not accept books that are not carried by distributors such as Baker & Taylor or Ingrams. He still did not want to incur the loss of income.

This was my second hardest new lesson, which led me to vow never to leave distribution decisions to an author's discretion, and to control my revenue stream instead of limiting its potential.

Without a budget for marketing, I mailed copies of books with press releases and synopses directly to buyers for consideration.

Next, I placed several books on consignment at independent bookstores, and used my public relations contacts to land on-air interviews on Urban Update on the NBC Affiliate Channel 7, WHDH TV. I also landed an article in Cambridge Chronicle.

Robert Peters was able to sell 70% of the 1,000 books printed within six months. Imagine what would be possible with a healthy marketing budget?

Da Goodie Monsta could have been in reproduction for second editions, in paperback and on high demand if it had been placed with a distributor with a healthy budget for marketing and publicity.

My ability to move ahead was limited because I was not earning a commission or revenue from sales efforts nor were many bookstores ordering.

In this economy, even a former printer of my paperback books had declared bankruptcy and closed its doors. I was forced to seek alternative methods to produce books with short runs. I decided to utilize on-demand printing sources and I discovered their print quality in most cases was comparable to the print vendor I had used to print paperback books.

Utilizing an on-demand printer freed up more funds for marketing and stacks of books in inventory weren't piling up in my house.

My decision to utilize on-demand printers was reinforced by the actions of a first-time author whose book I had spent $1,000 to print, and later she withdrew from the publishing contract within three months of signing because her expectations of being a bestseller or generating huge revenues had not been realized.

This author was under the impression that by having an online presence, her sales at Amazon must have been through the roof. She also didn't take into account the expense of organizing a book fair to sell her books.

The reality was that only one book had sold online, which was purchased by her sister. No sales occurred to generate revenues to cover printing costs or online marketing expenses. And I had to negotiate discount sales of the book with the bookstore that funded the book fair. My net profit was only $80 after working with her for three months.

This was my third hardest lesson to learn – to create contracts with terms long enough to ensure I can recoup my investments in a book. After losing money for printing and marketing this book, I realized I needed to add service terms to all my contracts. I decided to include two year terms of service to enable me to recoup my costs in publishing a book.

Posting of a book online does not guarantee sales. As a publisher, I had to establish procedures that would yield enough revenue to cover the production expenses for creating a book to make it a worthwhile venture for both the author and publisher.

Publishers are at the mercy of online agents to report sales and provide payments to them for books sold on their behalf. If the publisher isn't paid by bookstores, distributors and dealers, they likewise can't pay their authors a royalty.

This is why so many on-demand and self-publishing companies require authors to invest in themselves. It's like a reverse mortgage. You are paying an advance to the publisher who is banking on sales from your book. In the meantime, authors cover production costs until the revenue goals are reached.

As a result, online distributors cannot be the sole channel for sales. A combination of store placement, distribution, and direct marketing must also occur to increase sales.

There are more self-publishing enterprises than there are large commercial publishers that accept new authors. Few authors understand the industry and the level of promotional activity needed to increase visibility and generate sales.

These tough, eye-opening experiences did not deter me from my goal of sharing my experiences with others and of utilizing my skills to publish new writers. Instead, they taught me valuable lessons about what to do next.

As a small enterprise, I decided to contract with new writers who were just as new to publishing as I was so that we could grow together. I would issue books in paperback at no cost to the authors in exchange for a share of their royalties to offset the cost of production. I would take advantage of on-demand print services to lower my printing costs.

On-demand printing offers an added benefit: it is "Green" because it keeps the runs small in tandem with sales. This eliminates printing books that won't be sold.

Also, I decided to distribute books through electronic formats, like e-books, when applicable.

To defer other operational costs, I ask authors to pay for registering copyrights and for editing. And if they desire a hardcover book, they are required to pay a portion of the deposit paid to the printer, and in return are given 100 copies of their book.

For authors who commission their own artwork, I provide a free web page for online marketing as compensation for having signed Wiggles Press as their publisher. And I make an effort to highlight their activities in marketing.

Finding A Niche in Publishing Children's Books

When Wiggles Press pays for artwork, authors are required to contribute a small fee to any additional online marketing.

Wiggles Press has created an online community to bring authors together in a forum for sharing events, processes, and information.

http://wigglespress.ning.com

This is where editors, illustrators, and event planners are invited to join the community for promoting events and services related to publishing.

As a result of this new strategy, Wiggles Press has found a unique niche in publishing, and its collaboration with authors is growing. In fact, within six months, Wiggles Press has gone from publishing one author to having fifteen newly published writers on board.

The lessons learned through hardships have become the seeds to help me grow!

In conclusion, my goal is to collaborate with authors, illustrators, and editors to continue nurturing their ambitions as authors until eventually marketing efforts take root and we see the fruits of our labor blossom into revenue and sales.

Moreover, when Wiggles Press and its authorship become household names we will have fulfilled our mission of creating **books for the hands of little readers** that inspire them to read and learn with great joy and excitement.

Wiggle Room

WiggleRoom

Acknowledgments

This year has been filled with ups and downs and hurdles and miracles. I want to thank my Mom for always encouraging me to do my best and keep the faith. My children are an inspiration and my greatest joy. The people to whom I am most grateful are the illustrators and writers who have made Wiggles Press a reality and a collaborative enterprise from top to bottom.

First, I want to thank Mr. and Mrs. Peter McFarland who introduced me to Donald Cantor and Michael Cantor, authors of **The Perfect Pet**. Martin McDonald did a great job bringing this book to life.

Next, I want to thank Mel King for encouraging Robert Peters to bring me **Da Goodie Monsta** and trusting me to get it done for him. Robert, partner Earline and his family have been a publisher's dream come true from the very start.

Bill Young came along just as I got my second wind late in 2009 and has been the miracle I needed to keep going.

Al Margolis has been the icing on the cake with his humorous and color art, and most of all, his ever-supportive attitude toward my work. He created the new illustrations for the **Adventure of Gabe** series, and the cover of the book, **Presents for Phoebe**, and **Nanny Keys and Me**. He even created the cover of this book.

New artists who have launched their first books with me are Brian Dutton, Michelle Podgorski, and

Wiggle Room

Allison M. Healy. They have all brought a dimension to Wiggles Press that truly has made publishing a delight and joy.

Artisans Brittany Richardson, Berry Holly and Rosemarie Gillen came to me via authors, and have been equally embraced and valued as part of the Wiggles family.

My authors have all been blessed by the tireless work and dedication of editor Eugenie (Genie) Nakell for whom I will be forever grateful.

Authors for 2009 and 2010 have all contributed in some fashion to this work and my gratitude to them is endless: **Wiggle Room** contributors George P. Sommers, Jean Smith-Andrews, Monique Howard and Paula M. Ezop.

Thank you for joining Wiggles Press and I hope this will be a lifelong journey for us all.

Special heartfelt thanks to Emerson College Professor James Rowean for his review of this book and for his support of my goals.

Thank you, Larry Mayer for your review and contribution to the book.

WiggleRoom

wigglespress.com

Amazon.com

Barnes & Nobles

wiggleroom.wigglespress.com

www.ingramcontent.com/pod-product-compliance
Lightning Source LLC
Chambersburg PA
CBHW040512290326
R18043100001B/R180431PG41928CBX00002B/5